Ceremonies and Celebrations

GROWING UP

SUSAN BEHAR

HODDER

Books

Ceremonies and Celebrations

GROWING UP

Other titles in this series are:

BIRTHS • WEDDINGS • FEASTS AND FASTING
LIFE'S END • PILGRIMAGES AND JOURNEYS

Produced for Hodder Wayland by
Roger Coote Publishing
Gissing's Farm, Fressingfield
Suffolk IP21 5SH, UK

Published in Great Britain in 2000 by Hodder Wayland, an imprint of
Hodder Children's Books

© Hodder Wayland 2000

First published in paperback 2001

Editor: Alex Edmonds
Series Designer: Tim Mayer
Book Designer: Jane Hawkins

Consultants:
Khadijah Knight is a teacher and consultant on multicultural education
and Islam. She is also the author of several children's books about Islam.
Marcus Braybrooke is a parish priest and lecturer and writer on inter-
faith relations. He is joint President of the World Congress of Faiths.
Kanwaljit Kaur-Singh is a local authority inspector for education.
She has written many books on the Sikh tradition and appears on
television regularly.
Sharon Barron regularly visits schools to talk to children about Judaism.
She has written two books about Judaism for Hodder Wayland.
Meg St. Pierre is the Director of the Clear Vision Trust, a charitable
trust that aims to inform and educate about the teachings of the Buddha.
VP Hemant Kanitkar is a retired teacher and author of many books
on Hinduism.

Picture acknowledgements
Hutchison Library 11, 17 (Liba Taylor), 18, 22 (Liba Taylor), 23;
Panos Pictures *front cover* top left (Giacomo Pirozzi), *front cover* top
right (Neil Cooper), 10 (P Tweedie), 28 (John S Paull); Peter
Sanders 21; Tony Stone Images *front cover* bottom left (Bill Aron),
25 (Anthony Cassidy); Trip *front cover* bottom right (G Wittenberg),
1 (G Wittenberg), 4, (I Genut), 5 (Dinodia), 6 (M Fairman), 7 (F
Good), 8 (P Joseph), 9 (G Wittenberg), 12 (H Rogers), 13 (I Genut),
14 (H Rogers), 15 (H Rogers), 16 (H Rogers), 19, 20, 24 (Dinodia),
26 (A Gasson), 27 (J Batten), 29 (T Bognar).

A Catalogue record for this book is available from the
British Library.
ISBN 0 7502 3308 7

Printed and bound in Italy by G. Canale & C. S.p.A. Turin, Italy

Hodder Children's Books
a division of Hodder Headline Limited
338 Euston Road, London NW1 3BH

CONTENTS

Becoming an Adult   4

The Christian Tradition   6

The Jewish Tradition   10

The Sikh Tradition   14

The Muslim Tradition   18

The Hindu Tradition   22

The Buddhist Tradition   26

Glossary   30

Further Information   31

Index   32

Becoming an Adult

In many countries across the world, children and their families mark and celebrate the stage in their lives when they are ready to become an adult member of their religion or to make a commitment to it. These ceremonies are usually known as initiation ceremonies, and the young people are called initiates.

Different religions have different customs and ceremonies to mark a person's initiation, although most take place around the ages of 12 to 13, when it is believed a child can understand enough about his or her religion to know whether or not to follow its laws and customs. In some religions, however, such as Islam, a newborn baby automatically belongs to the parents' religion.

In religions such as Judaism, initiates prepare for their entrance into the faith by learning religious texts. ▼

Special services

The services that mark the occasions are different in each religion. However, many of the ceremonies require the initiate to have had special lessons to learn about the customs, beliefs and laws of his or her religion. In some cases, the initiate will read a passage from the scriptures and, in order to do so, may have had to learn a foreign language. For example, a Sikh in America or the UK must learn to read the *Guru Granth Sahib* (the Sikh scriptures) in Punjabi, a language that originally comes from India.

And in all of the religions we look at, the families of the initiates play an important part in supporting their children before, and often during, the ceremony.

These special days mark an important step in a young person's life and are occasions of great joy for all concerned.

Parents of the initiate very often guide him or her in the traditions of the faith. ▼

Different customs across the world

Initiation ceremonies for the same religion can vary from country to country. For example, a Roman Catholic confirmation in Spain may differ from a Roman Catholic confirmation in Britain in that female candidates from Spain usually wear special white dresses with veils, whereas in Britain they will often just wear ordinary smart clothes.

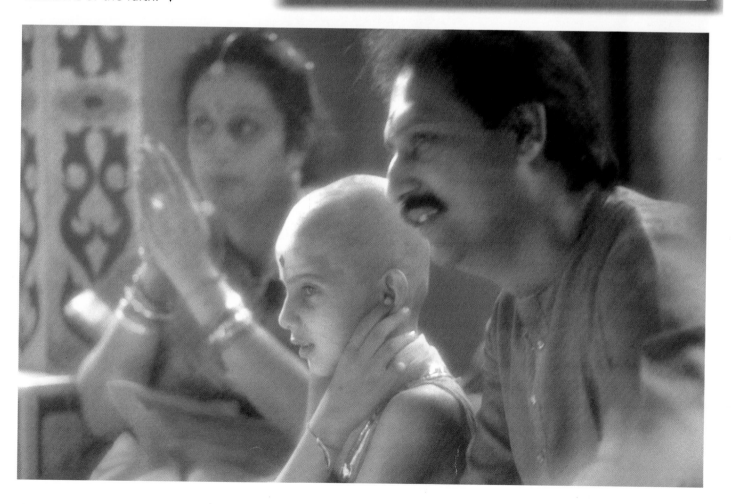

The Christian Tradition

Christians have two ceremonies to welcome a person into the faith; baptism and confirmation.

Baptism is when a person first becomes part of the Christian family, and many Christian parents have their babies baptised when they are just a few months old. The ceremony takes place in a church with friends, family and godparents present. From that point on, and throughout a child's early years, Christian parents may try to help their child to become a Christian in many different ways. He or she may be encouraged to read Bible stories, go to church every Sunday and celebrate Christian rituals, such as giving up something they enjoy at Lent or distributing food to the elderly at the Harvest festival.

▲ At Sunday school, children talk about passages from the Bible and what they mean. The classes often involve a lot of singing and listening to Bible stories.

A child's first Communion is a special occasion. Family and friends attend the service and photographs are taken as souvenirs. ▶

Sunday school

Once the child is old enough to understand the Bible and Christian prayers, he or she may go to Sunday school or Bible classes. There children hear about Jesus and his teachings. They learn how a true Christian should behave. When children are old enough and understand what being a Christian means, they are asked if they want to confirm their faith and the vows that were made for them when they were baptised. This ceremony is known as confirmation.

Holy Communion

Catholic children have their First Holy Communion when they are about 7. They are then confirmed when they are 13. Protestant children cannot take Communion until they are confirmed at age 13. At Communion, a small piece of bread and a sip of wine which have been blessed by a priest are given to each worshipper. For Christians, the bread represents Jesus's body and the wine represents his blood. This is the way that they remember Jesus's life and death. It reminds Christians of the last meal Jesus shared with his disciples – the Last Supper.

Faye's story

'My name is Faye and I was confirmed when I was 14. On the day of my confirmation I was very excited. Although I had been taking Communion for seven years, confirmation is an important occasion.

I was confirmed with 20 other children from my parish. The ceremony started like the usual service. After the reading from the Gospel, the names of everyone making a confirmation were called out and he or she stood up. Then we went up to the altar to be anointed with oil. Afterwards we all had our photos taken along with the Bishop.'

The ceremony

▲ Young candidates receive their first Eucharist – bread and wine that symbolizes the body and blood of Christ – at the confirmation service.

In the Anglican and Roman Catholic branches of Christianity, most children are confirmed at the age of 13, although the ceremony can take place at any time after this and into adulthood. In Orthodox Christianity (the traditional Eastern European Christian religion), a child is automatically confirmed when he or she is baptised as a baby. For several months before a ceremony, the confirmation candidate will go to a special class to learn about the ceremony and what it means to be a Christian. The service is conducted by the Bishop in a church and several candidates will be confirmed at the same time. At the ceremony, the Bishop asks each candidate to make his or her own baptismal promises. He asks them whether they repent of their sins and they have to reply 'yes'. Then he asks them if they 'turn to Christ' and again they have to answer 'yes'.

The candidate kneels before the Bishop who lays his hands on the candidate's head. The Bishop then confirms the candidate in the Christian faith, speaking aloud his or her name and saying, 'Confirm, O Lord, your servant with your Holy Spirit'.

The laying on of hands is a tradition which goes back to the early days of the Church, when Jesus laid his hands on his disciples' heads. In the Roman Catholic tradition each confirmation candidate is anointed with oil, called the chrism, on the forehead.

After the ceremony

After being confirmed, the candidates usually have a celebration, such as a family meal or party. The godparents, who were chosen by the child's parents to support him or her throughout life, usually attend both the ceremony and the celebration and give special gifts to the child so that he or she will remember this special day.

Sacred text

Jesus taught that people should be like children if they want to go to heaven. By this he meant that they should be innocent and pure rather than that they should act childishly. 'Let the children come to me... for the Kingdom of God belongs to such as these. I tell you, whoever does not accept the Kingdom of God like a child will never enter it.'

The Bible: Mark 10:13

◄ *The white dresses that the female initiates wear symbolize purity.*

The Jewish Tradition

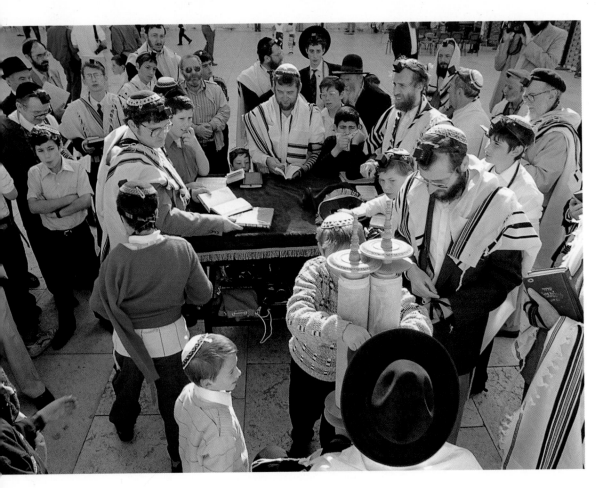

◄ *For his* bar mitzvah, *a boy usually has to learn the entire Haftarah section of the Torah, containing the writings of the Prophets. The boy in this picture is carrying the Torah scrolls to be read at a table.*

When Jewish boys are 13 years old and girls are 12 years old, they can become adults in the eyes of the Jewish religion by taking part in a special ceremony. For boys this is called a *bar mitzvah*, which means Son of the Commandments, and for girls, *bat mitzvah*, which means Daughter of the Commandments.

The Commandments are the laws that Jews must follow. Jews believe that God gave the laws to Moses, the Jewish prophet, over 2,000 years ago. Both boys and girls need to prepare for the ceremony, which involves reading a passage from the *Torah* in Hebrew in front of friends and family in the synagogue. It can take over a year to prepare for this and have a good understanding of the scriptures.

The Torah *contains the first five books of the Bible: Genesis, Exodus, Leviticus, Numbers and Deuteronomy.* ▶

Sarah's story

'I'm Sarah. At my brother David's *bar mitzvah* I sat with my mother and aunts. David was very nervous when he read out aloud from the *Torah* in Hebrew. The next day we had a large party at a hotel. My father made a speech saying how proud he was of David. We were all proud. My *bat mitzvah* is next year, when I'm 12 years old, and I am already going to Hebrew classes.'

The *Torah* is the most important of the Jewish scriptures and it is where their laws and customs, and Bible stories, are written. It is written in Hebrew, the ancient language of the Jewish people. To learn Hebrew, Jewish children attend a special religious school called a *Cheder* from an early age. In the *Cheder* children learn what it means to be a Jew, how and why the Jews believe in one God and the laws that they must obey.

At the *bar mitzvah*, the boy wears traditional clothes for the first time, including a *tallit* (a prayer shawl) and a *kippah* (cap) on his head. The ceremony takes place during the normal *Shabbat* (Saturday) service in the synagogue. The boy waits near the *bimah*, a platform from where the *Torah* is read. The *Torah* is stored inside the *Ark*, and at the beginning of the service, it is taken from the *Ark* and placed on the *bimah*. The boy is called to the *bimah* to read the passage he has learnt. Nobody is allowed to touch the sacred scrolls, so a special pointer called a *yad* is used to help follow the words. Afterwards the rabbi, the Jewish teacher, blesses the boy.

After the ceremony

Afterwards the boy will have a party or celebratory meal with his friends and family. He will be given presents. At the meal, he'll thank his parents for their support and help.

What does bar mitzvah mean?

When a boy has had his *bar mitzvah*, he becomes an adult in the eyes of the Jewish community. At the ceremony he confirms his commitment to Judaism when he says: 'In the *Torah* I have read the word of God. With your help may I go on to fulfil it in my life. Amen.' Now he can be counted as one of the ten men needed to make up the number required for a service to take place in a synagogue. He will also be expected to act as an adult at religious services, so, for example, he will fast on the festival of *Yom Kippur*.

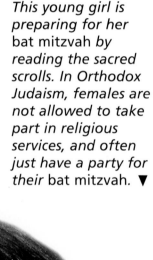

This young girl is preparing for her bat mitzvah *by reading the sacred scrolls. In Orthodox Judaism, females are not allowed to take part in religious services, and often just have a party for their* bat mitzvah. ▼

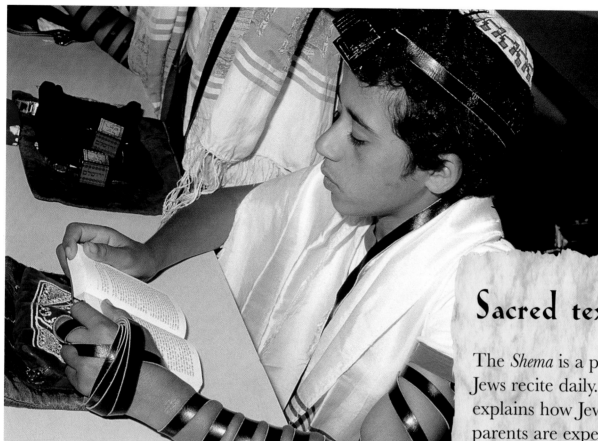

▲ *This young boy is praying. He wears* tefillin, *a box containing religious texts that is tied around the hands for morning prayers. Only boys over the age of 13 can wear* tefillin.

Bat mitzvah

Girls have a *bat mitzvah* when they are 12 years old. Fewer girls than boys celebrate their coming-of-age. In both *bat* and *bar mitzvahs*, the ceremonies may differ, depending upon whether they are in the Orthodox (traditional) or Reform (modern) tradition. In the Orthodox tradition, a *bat mitzvah* usually takes place on a Sunday and the girls do not read from the *Torah*.

Sacred text

The *Shema* is a prayer that Jews recite daily. It explains how Jewish parents are expected to teach their religion to their children.

'Love the Lord your God with all your heart, and with all your soul and with all your strength. And these words, which I am commanding you today, shall be upon your heart. And you shall teach them carefully to your children.'

The Bible: Deuteronomy 6: 4–9

The Sikh Tradition

▲ The father of this young boy is tying the small *patka* turban around the boy's head and over his uncut hair.

An important moment in a young Sikh's life is when he or she enters the *Khalsa*, the Sikh 'family' or 'community', and agrees to follow the teachings of the Sikh religion.

The ceremony that marks this occasion is called *Amrit*. Sikhs can take part in this ceremony at any time in their lives, although usually they are at least 14 years old, or are old enough to understand what they are promising and committing themselves to. The ceremony takes place in the *gurdwara*, the Sikh place of worship, where the Sikh scriptures, the *Guru Granth Sahib*, are kept.

Sikhs believe that God's truth is revealed through the *Guru Granth Sahib*, which is written in Punjabi, a language originating in India. This means that Sikhs all over the world learn Punjabi and children must be able to read and recite it for the *Amrit* ceremony. The *Guru Granth Sahib* teaches the main Sikh beliefs: that Sikhs should always remember God, earn their living honestly and share with other people, especially those in need. It also teaches children to respect their parents and to care for them in old age. The family is very important to Sikhs and it is often the parents who teach their children about Sikh history and culture.

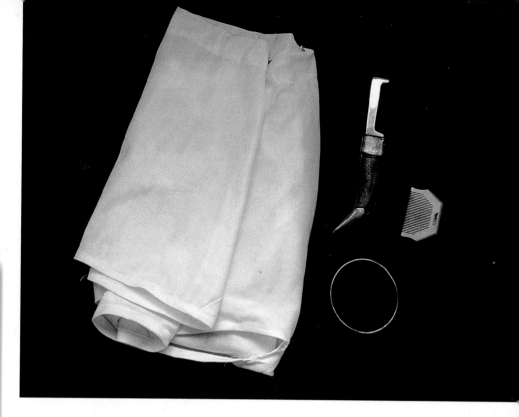

Four of the five Ks are shown here: the bracelet (kara), the small sword (kirpan), the comb (kangha) and the shorts (kachera). ▶

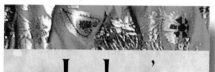

Jasdeep's story

'My name is Jasdeep and I'm 14. I was nervous about taking my *Amrit*, but my parents encouraged me and helped me learn the words of the *Ardas* prayer. When it happened I was worried that I hadn't recited the words of the prayer properly, but afterwards my parents said that the most important thing to remember was that I was wholehearted about wanting to be part of the Sikh family.'

The five Ks

When a Sikh has his *Amrit*, he must wear the Five Ks. These take their name from the first letter of the Punjabi words for them. The five Ks are:

- *kara:* a steel bracelet, which represents the person's devotion to God;
- *kirpan:* a small sword, which symbolizes the person's willingness to defend the weak;
- *kesh:* uncut hair, which symbolizes strength;
- *kangha:* a comb, to represent cleanliness;
- *kachera:* shorts, which symbolize purity.

The patka

Sikh men and some boys don't cut their hair. To keep it neat, they wear it in a turban. Instead of wearing a full turban – which is made from a long piece of fabric, wound around the head in a special way – young boys can wear a small turban, called a *patka*. Or sometimes a boy simply plaits his uncut hair and ties it at the back of his head.

This picture shows the founding of the Khalsa, when five Punjabi men first prepared the amrit*, to baptise Guru Gobind Singh, the 10th Sikh guru.* ▶

The ceremony

Wearing the five Ks, the initiates go to the *Khalsa*, where five fully initiated Sikhs conduct the service. They are also wearing the five Ks. At the beginning of the ceremony the responsibilities of being a Sikh are explained to the initiates.

The initiates agree to these obligations, which include praying five times a day and serving other people. Prayers are said and the *amrit* is prepared. *Amrit* is a mixture of sugar and water and represents the sweetness and holiness of God. When it is ready, it is poured into the cupped hands of each of the initiates for them to drink. This is repeated five times and then it is sprinkled over their eyes and into their hair five times. Then the *Mool Mantar,* the first words of the *Guru Granth Sahib,* is recited and the new initiates are given their Sikh names. All boys are given the last name Singh, meaning 'lion', and girls, the last name Kaur, meaning 'princess'.

Sacred text

The *Mool Mantar* is recited by the new initiates. When the initiates read this, they are publicly accepting the Sikh religion.

'There is one and only one God
Whose name is Truth
God the Creator is without fear, without hate, immortal, without form and is beyond birth and death
And is understood through God's Grace.'

*Guru Granth Sahib:
The Mool Mantar*

Sikhs see the Guru Granth Sahib as the head of their religion. It contains the words of the founders of Sikhism as well as writings from people of other faiths. ▶

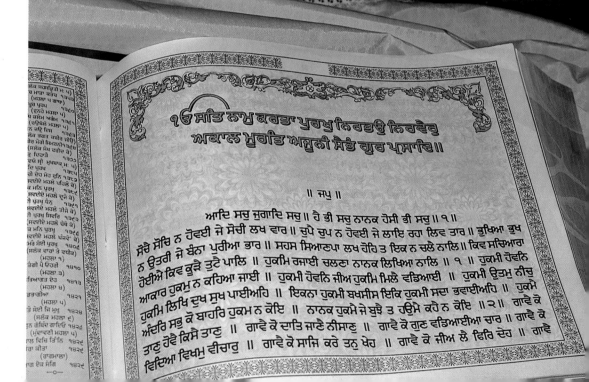

The Muslim Tradition

▲ *Every Muslim boy must learn to read and respect the Qur'an. It contains the Word of God (Allah) which was written down by the Prophet Muhammad (Peace Be Upon Him).*

In Islam, a baby is automatically a member of the Islamic faith, so there are no special initiation ceremonies. However a few days after a male child is born, the *Adhan* (the Muslim call to prayer) is whispered to him. From an early age, Muslim children go to the mosque to learn about their religion. They also start to learn to read the Qur'an in Arabic at special lessons after school or at weekends.

Bismallah

In India, Muslims have a ceremony called *Bismallah*, which takes place when a child is four years, four months and four weeks old. This ceremony marks the beginning of the child's religious education and is the first time that he or she will learn to read the Qur'an. It commemorates the first time that the Angel Jibril appeared to Muhammad (Peace Be Upon Him) to deliver Allah's message.

The child's father and friends come to the house and the father teaches the child the first lesson from the Qur'an, which begins: 'In the name of Allah the most gracious, the most merciful'. The child is taught some verses from the Qur'an, and then everyone celebrates and eats sweetmeats (sweet cakes).

By the time Muslim children are seven years old, they are taught how to perform the *Salah* (the Muslim prayers) and to understand the Five Pillars of Islam (the duties of a Muslim). By the time a child reaches puberty, he or she is expected to carry out religious duties, such as praying five times a day.

Muslim children are taught self-respect and respect for others, as well as how to be charitable by sharing food with neighbours and people in need. The family is the very centre of Muslim life and parents and children are taught in the Qur'an to care for each other.

Sacred text ☾⋆

These are the words of the *Shahadah*, the prayer that a Muslim says when he or she chooses Islam as a way of life.

'There is no God but Allah.
Muhammad is the Messenger of Allah'.

The Pillars of Islam: The First Pillar

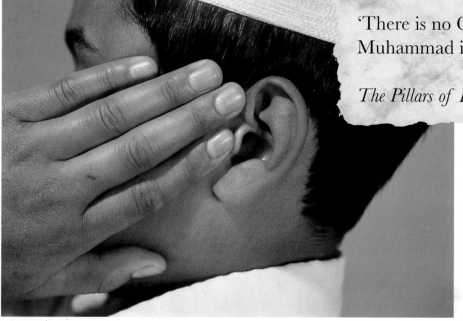

◄ *Muslim boys must learn to pray five times a day. At the start of a prayer, Muslims raise both hands to their ears as a sign of respect to Allah.*

The Five Pillars

The five main duties for Muslims are called the Five Pillars of Islam. When Muslim children reach puberty, they are expected to follow these duties. They must recite the *Shahadah*, the Muslim confession of faith. Every Muslim must also pray five times a day. This is known as the *Salah*. Prayers are recited in Arabic and accompanied by body movements, such as kneeling and bowing. The Third Pillar is *Zakah*, which means purification. To follow this duty, Muslims give some of their income to charity. Every year 2.5 per cent of a family's income that is left over after paying all their bills is given to charity. Muslims must also fast during the month of *Ramadan*. The fast is known as *Sawm*. The fifth and final Pillar of Islam is every Muslim's duty to go on a pilgrimage once in his or her lifetime, to Makkah in Saudi Arabia. This is known as *Hajj*.

When Muslim children reach puberty, they can go on a pilgrimage. ▼

▲ Young Muslims are taught that when they pray, they must face towards Makkah, the birthplace of the Prophet Muhammad (pbuh).

Homaa's story

'This is the first time I've fasted at *Ramadan*, now that I am ten. For the first few days I got very tired because I hadn't eaten all day. I'd get up early before sunrise and eat breakfast with my family, but before dawn, we'd all stop eating until the end of the day at sunset. It was summer and very hot all day, so my parents made sure that I drank lots of water in the morning. At the end of the day, we break the fast with a big meal and we always have a pinch of salt, some dates and milk and honey with it.'

The Qur'an

The Qur'an is the holy book of the Muslims and Muslim children must learn from it. It is written in Arabic and it is believed to be the Word of God (Allah) revealed to Muhammad (pbuh), a prophet of Islam. Muslims believe that God talked to Muhammad who then told his disciples exactly what God had said. The disciples wrote down God's words and they are now in the Qur'an. The Qur'an gives Muslims guidance on Islamic belief, law and customs. Parts of it are regularly recited in prayers. Wherever a Muslim lives in the world, he or she always recites the Qur'an in Arabic.

The Hindu Tradition

Between the ages of 8 and 14, many Hindu boys take part in a ceremony that begins the *Brahmacharya* or student stage of their life. This is one of the four stages in a Hindu's life. The others are *Grihastha*, the stage when a Hindu is married and working; *Vanaprastha* when a Hindu is retired; and *Sannyasa*, an optional stage for men only, who have fulfilled their family responsibilities and can then spend their lives praying and meditating.

The ceremony to mark the *Brahmacharya* is called the *Upanayana*, or the sacred thread ceremony. It represents the boy's spiritual rather than earthly birth, called his second birth (*dvija*). It means that he is a full member of the Hindu religion and as such he is allowed to hear, learn and recite the *Vedas* and other scriptures. He can also now represent the family in worship. Most boys will begin to learn Sanskrit (the sacred language of the Hindu scriptures) when they are about five years old. By the time they reach adolescence, it is believed they are old enough to understand the faith. This is when *Upanayana* takes place.

At the sacred thread ceremony, tradition says that money must change hands between the young man and any of his sisters. ▼

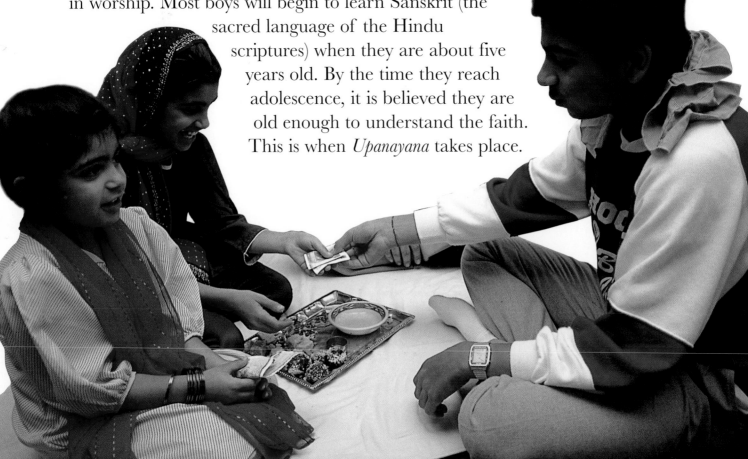

The Vedas

The *Vedas* are the scriptures of the Hindu faith. *Veda* means 'knowledge' in Sanskrit. They contain hymns to the many gods of the Hindus, as well as stories and poems about them. They were written over 3,000 years ago. The first and most important of the *Vedas* is the *Rig Veda* (Royal Veda). At the *Upanayana* ceremony, the boy will be taught its most sacred verse, the *Gayatri*, for the first time.

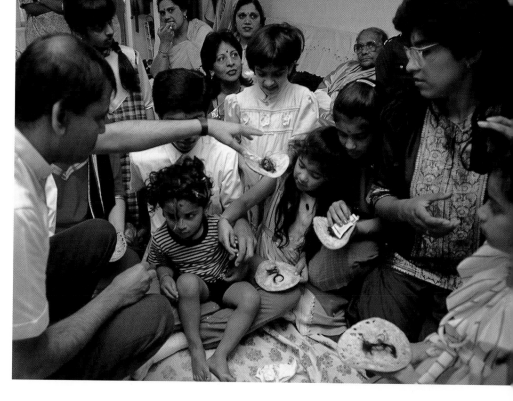

▲ *Initiation ceremonies for young boys may involve them having their hair cut. The family keeps locks of the boy's hair.*

Hindu classes and castes

Hindu society is divided into four main classes, or *Varnas*. Each class represents certain members of society, such as priests or professionals (*Brahmins*), soldiers and administrators (*Kshatriyas*), businessmen and farmers (*Vaishyas*) and artisans (*Shudras*). Traditionally the classes cannot intermarry, although today many mixed marriages do take place. Each class is then subdivided into many castes. Only boys from the *Brahmin*, *Vaishya* and *Kshatriya* classes have the *Upanayana* ceremony.

Viran's story

'Before my *Upanayana* I had my hair cut and I put on my best silk clothes. Then I had to change into white cotton clothes along with the other boys also taking *Upanayana*. These clothes symbolize cleanliness and rebirth. After the ceremony we had an enormous meal with lots of my family there. Some of them I had never met before, but they had come from India because it was such a special day.'

The ceremony

The ceremony usually takes place at home. Family, friends and Hindu priests – known as *Brahmins* because only people from the *Brahmin* caste can be priests – are present. Before the ceremony, the initiate may have his head completely shaved or just have his hair clipped. During the ceremony, he changes his clothes and puts on a simple cotton garment to wear. Then he is given the sacred thread and told, 'Now you are a man'. The sacred thread is a loop with three strands of strong cotton and is worn on the left shoulder, across the chest and back, and hanging below the right hand. The strands represent the first three *Vedas,* and also three important Hindu gods, *Brahma* (the creator), *Vishnu* (the protector) and *Shiva* (the destroyer). Traditionally, the initiate should wear the sacred thread every day, but today, most Hindus will only wear it on special occasions.

▲ *The name* Upanayana *means 'to lead a child near'. This means that the child is led near to the guru, a holy man who understands the scriptures. An understanding of the scriptures is said to prevent Godlessness.*

Sacred text

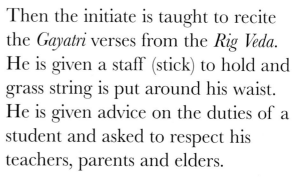

These words from the *Gayatri* mantra are recited every day by Hindus.

'We meditate on the glory and brilliance of the Sun God which lights up the heavens and the Earth. May he bless us and inspire us.'

Rig Veda: Gayatri mantra

Then the initiate is taught to recite the *Gayatri* verses from the *Rig Veda*. He is given a staff (stick) to hold and grass string is put around his waist. He is given advice on the duties of a student and asked to respect his teachers, parents and elders.

Many years ago in India, where Hinduism came from, the end of the ceremony would have been different. The boy would have actually left home to study with a *guru* (religious teacher). These days the boy only pretends to leave home. In reality he stays at home and shares a big meal with his family and friends.

◄ *Young boys may wear yellow-coloured turbans at their initiation ceremonies. This is because yellow is thought to bring good luck.*

The Buddhist Tradition

The Buddha was a prince called Siddhartha Gautama, who lived in India in the sixth century BC and who came to be known as the Buddha or Enlightened One. His teachings are known as the *Dharma* and are found in the Buddhist scriptures. The Buddha taught that people can find Enlightenment if they follow his teachings. Enlightenment is described by the Buddha as being in a very happy and peaceful state. There are no specific ceremonies that initiate a young person into the Buddhist tradition, but they may be taught to meditate to bring them closer to Enlightenment. To be a Buddhist, you need to live in a way that is in keeping with the teachings of the Buddha. Many Buddhist parents in the West allow their children to choose whether or not they wish to become a Buddhist. In eastern countries, such as Tibet and China, Buddhism is much more traditional and widely followed. Very often children can even join Buddhist monasteries to strengthen their faith.

A monk tutors a young initiate in Buddhist scriptures at a monastery in Bumtang, Bhutan. ▶

Joining a monastery

Boys can enter a monastery to study with the monks at any age, although most wait until they are about ten years old. The young boy is known as a novice monk. When a novice enters the monastery, he recites the mantra of the Three Jewels. Buddhists may recite the Jewels daily to remind them to put their faith in the Buddha, the *Dharma* (teachings) and the *Sangha* (monastery), rather than in the world.

The novice shaves his head (this symbolizes a fresh start) and changes out of his usual clothes into an orange robe. Most monks wear orange robes made from simple material. This is because the first followers of the Buddha wore rags stitched together and stained with mud, which turned them a yellow-orange colour. Once in the monastery, the novice will live a very similar life to a fully trained monk. He will, for example, help with tasks in the monastery, such as cleaning. The novice will have lessons in Buddhism and other subjects such as maths. He will also spend time meditating with the other monks. Girls can also enter a nunnery for a period of time as novice nuns.

▲ *One of the most important things that a young monk must learn is how to pray.*

Nagamudra's story

'When my parents said goodbye to me at the monastery, I felt very unhappy and didn't want to be left in this strange place. But I soon got to know the other boys and made friends. The monks were kind to me and helped me with my reading and other lessons. Although I enjoyed the experience, I didn't see my parents for four months and I was happy to go home to see my family and taste my mother's cooking again.'

Meditation

Buddhists believe that regular meditation helps people to find Enlightenment, so Buddhists learn to meditate from an early age. Most Buddhists meditate for a short time every day, but monks and nuns sometimes meditate for many hours at a time. When Buddhists meditate they sit on the floor, usually on a cushion, close their eyes, and quieten their minds. This is more difficult than it sounds. Followers of the Buddha are expected to follow five rules, known as the Five Precepts or promises. These promises are taught to young Buddhists. They are:

- not to kill anything that breathes;
- not to take anything which is not given;
- not to harm people through sexual behaviour;
- not to lie;
- not to drink alcohol.

When a young monk meditates, he must empty his mind of everyday thoughts. ▼

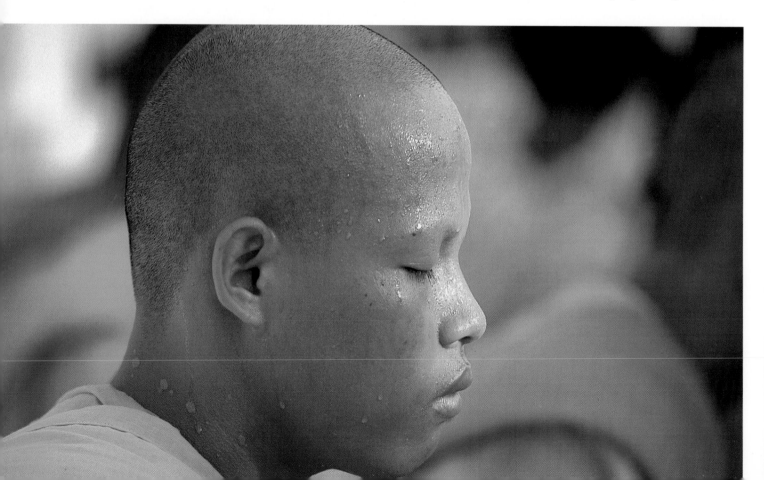

◀ *Buddhist children, like this young nun, are taught to follow the teachings of the Buddha and to live a harmless and good life.*

Sacred text

These words from the Three Jewels (see page 27) show that Buddhists trust the teachings of the Buddha.

'I go to the Buddha for refuge
I go to the *Dharma* for refuge
I go to the *Sangha* for refuge.'

Pali Canon: The Three Jewels

Theravada and Mahayana traditions

There are two main types of Buddhism. In some countries, such as Vietnam, Thailand and Burma, Buddhists follow the *Theravada* tradition, whilst in China, Tibet and Japan, they follow the *Mahayana* tradition. Each tradition has different customs and beliefs. For example, in some countries, such as Burma, there is a special ceremony for when a novice enters a monastery. The young boy dresses up in fine silk clothes and rides to the monastery on a horse. When he reaches the monastery he changes into simple clothes and has his head shaved. This ritual remembers the time the Buddha began his spiritual life, when he gave up the riches he had as a prince to become a holy man.

GLOSSARY

Adhan the Muslim call to prayer, made five times a day from the mosque.

Allah the Muslim word for God.

amrit literally means 'nectar'. It is made by stirring sugar into a bowl of water and is used at Sikh ceremonies.

Amrit the ceremony that marks a young Sikh's entry into the Sikh community.

Bible the holy book of the Christians.

bimah the platform in a synagogue where the *Torah* is read.

Cheder a school in which Jewish children are taught Jewish history, principles and customs.

Enlightenment literally meaning 'realising the truth'. The state of tranquillity that Buddhists aspire to by following the teachings of the Buddha.

faith a belief in a religion or idea.

Gospel the teachings of Jesus Christ.

gurdwara a Sikh place of worship.

guru a Sikh leader.

Heaven in Christianity, where God is believed to live and where good Christians go after they have died.

Judaism the traditional form of Judaism follows the teachings of the *Torah* strictly.

Makkah the holy city of Muslims where the Prophet Muhammad (pbuh) was born.

mantra a word or phrase that is repeated to help people concentrate when they are meditating.

monastery a place where monks live and worship.

mosque a Muslim place of worship.

Orthodox traditional forms of religion.

Peace Be Upon Him (pbuh) the standard phrase that is repeated after the name of an Islamic prophet is spoken, as a mark of respect.

prophet someone who foretells things about a religion.

Punjabi a language spoken in the Punjab, an area that is split between India and Pakistan.

Qur'an the Muslim holy book.

rabbi a leader of the Jewish faith.

Ramadan the Muslim month of fasting from dawn to dusk.

Reform Judaism a more modern form of Judaism than the Orthodox tradition.

Sangha generally the community of Buddhists. It can also mean the community within a monastery.

scriptures holy writings.

Sanskrit an ancient Indian language used in the Hindu scriptures.

symbolize to represent something.

synagogue a Jewish place of worship.

Torah the holy book of the Jews.

Upanayana the ceremony for Hindu boys that marks the beginning of the student stage of life.

Yom Kippur literally 'Day of Atonement'. A Jewish festival which involves fasting.

FURTHER INFORMATION

Books

Beliefs and Cultures: Christian by Carol Watson,
Watts, 1996.

Islam (World Religions) by Khadijah Knight,
Wayland, 1995.

Islam (World Religions) by Richard Tames,
Watts, 1999.

What do we know about Buddhism? by Anita Ganeri,
Macdonald Young Books, 1997.

The Jewish World by Douglas Charing,
Simon and Schuster Young Books, 1992.

Hinduism (World Religions) by Katherine Prior,
Watts, 1999.

What do we know about Hinduism? by Anita Ganeri,
Macdonald Young Books, 1995.

Sikhism (World Religions) by Kanwaljit Kaur-Singh,
Wayland, 1995.

What I Believe (Discover the Religions of the World)
by Alan Brown and Andrew Langley,
Macdonald Young Books, 1999.

Websites

education@clear-vision.org – The website for the Clear Vision Trust, a
project that provides Buddhist resources.

http://www.sikhfoundation.org/ – The Sikh Foundation.

http://www.hindusamajtemple.org/ht/hindu.html –
An introduction to Hinduism.

http://www.islamicity.org/ – An introduction to the world of Islam.

http://conline.net/ – Christians Online, a Christian resource.

http://www.jewishweb.com/ – The Worldwide Jewish Web.

INDEX

All the numbers in **bold** refer to photographs

Allah 18, 19, 21, 30
amrit **16**, 17, 30
Amrit 14, 15, 30
Ark 11

baptism 6
bar mitzvah **10**, 11, 12, 13
bat mitzvah 10, **12**, 13
Bible 6, 7, 9, 11, 13, 30
bimah 11, 30
Bishops 7, 8
Brahmins 23, 24
Buddha 26, 27, 28, 29

castes 23, 24
Cheder 11, 30
chrism 9
churches 6, 7
clothes 5, 9, 23, 24, 27, 29
Communion 7
confirmation 6, 7, 8

families 4, 10, 12, 14, 15, 22
fasting 20

gurdwaras 14, 30
Guru Granth Sahib 4, 14, **17**
gurus 24, 30

Hebrew 11

India 14, 23, 25, 26
initiates **4**, 5, 16, 17, **26**

Jesus 7
Jibril, Angel 18

kachera **15**
kangha **15**
kara **15**
kesh 15
khalsa 14, 16
kippah 11
kirpan **15**

laws 4, 10, 11, 21

Makkah 20, 21, 30
mantras 23, 30
marriage 22, 23
meditation 25, 26, 28
monks **26**, 27
Moses 10
mosques 18, 30

Orthodox faiths 8, 12, 13, 30

parents 5, 6, 12, 13, 14, 15, 17, 21, 25, 26, 27
pilgrimages **20**
prayers 7, **13**, 15, 17, 19, 20
Prophet Muhammad (pbuh) 18, 19, 21

Punjabi 4, 14, 16

Qur'an **18**, 21, 30

rabbis 11
Ramadan 20, 21, 30
Roman Catholicism 5

sacred thread ceremony **22**, **24**
Sanskrit 22, 23, 30
scriptures 4, 10, 24, 26, 30
Shabbat 11
singing 6
synagogues 10, 11, 12, 30

tallit 11
tefellin 13
Torah 10, 11, 12, 13, 30
turbans **14**, 15, **25**

Upanayana 22, 23, 24, 30

Vedas 22, 23, 24, 25

yad 11
Yom Kippur 12, 30